To Zara Ann Taylo

We wrote this book together,
long before you could even read!

Who knows where this life will take you!

All my love,

Poppop

Illustrations by yami-digital

Cover design by John Weisman

I love it when you read to me!

The words you say can help me see

This great big world that we live in,

and the discovering I will soon begin!

Sitting here right now with you,

thumbing through pages like we do,

helps to cultivate my mind

and prepare me for the world I'll find!

Every window and every door

leads to places I'll explore!

Near and far, here and there,

we'll find places everywhere—

places we will often go,

places I can't wait to know;

places where we sleep and eat,

places up and down our street;

at the park and in the store,

endless places to explore;

in the country and in the town;

so many places to be found!

This world must hold so many surprises,

all different colors, all shapes and sizes!

How can there be so many places
all spread out in different spaces?

Someday I'll grow big like you

and discover things that I can do!

I'll crawl, and walk, and run, and play,

and keep exploring every day!

But until then, I'm happy here

offering you my listening ear!

So keep on reading like you do

for my favorite place is here with you!

Made in the USA
Monee, IL
29 January 2021